In Case I Never Told You

by:

Ashleigh Peroney

To My 'Why'

To my mom, the one who taught me the importance of seeing things through; the one who taught me life isn't always going to be pretty—you taught me it's always worth living. You taught me nothing worth having is just handed to you. You were tough on me because you saw my potential. You were the one who wouldn't take, "I'm tried", as an excuse to quit; the one who let me cry it all out, but told me to wipe those tears just as quickly.

To my family, the ones who showed me the definition of strength and who taught me the shirt off your own back could mean the world to someone else.

To my friends, the ones that brought the smiles out to cover up the tears and who picked me up every time I fell.

To My Readers

This is a collection of my thoughts and true feelings. I wrote each letter specific to the person, situation, or thing it is about. Something so specific to me can be so vague to you, while at the same time being so specific to you and your life.

Some of these letters will hit home. If not personally, maybe these demons have affected you indirectly.

We all suffer from the same pains, just in different variations. Some of these letters will take you back to things you may have wanted to forget. Though in my case, I wrote these letters to help me face my demons, as a way of confronting everything I never could. After each letter, I have left a section for

'Self-Reflection'. I left this section because I feel it is important for you all to face your demons and confront the people, situations, and things you have been suppressing. Use this section. Write your own story, perspectives, or just jot down some notes.

In case I never told you, it's YOUR turn to heal.

To My Story

One tear turned to two; two tears turned to three; three tears turned into a full-on breakdown.

Blankets became tissues and pillows became sound boxes keeping it all hidden.

Self-pity, regret, and depression filled me. Questions of "How did it get this far?", "Why can't I make it stop?", "Will the feeling ever go away?" they repeat in my head, playing back louder and louder.

Is this my punishment? What must I do to make it stop?

Looking into the bathroom mirror I debated on resorting to my old solution. The thought of it getting that dark again just makes me cry even more.

Peering up from the pillow and seeing my reflection in the mirror, seeing me at my lowest, made me realize I need to pick myself back up. Refusing to let myself slip again, I sat there for a second and realized there was so much more that brought me to this point.

I thought about the situation that triggered this episode. I needed to let out the truth. I needed to stop protecting others' feelings by putting all of the burden on myself.

If I could tell you about all the people and things that brought me to my lowest point, the truthful and raw thoughts, where would I be? If I took the time to face these people and things, would I find my peace?

In the end, I grabbed a pencil and paper and wrote down the first sentence—'In case I never told you...'

Before long, one sentence turned to two; two turned to three; three turned into a full letter.

At the end of the letter, I confronted my first demon. I was finally able to write out all the thoughts that I had bottled up deep inside. I hadn't realized it was a demon until the emotions continued pouring out, unstoppable.

One letter turned to two; two letters turned to three; three letters turned into thirty-six.

I started confronting demon after demon. Before long, my diary turned into my therapist.

My words became confessions; confessing all the pain and hurt I had allowed these demons to put me through and how much of their blame I'd put on myself. It wasn't long before I was confessing the things I had suppressed all this time.

It wasn't until I finished the letter that I realized the actual impact these demons had on me. For so long, I gave my power away to so many people and situations that weren't deserving of it.

My lowest point, the reflection in the mirror, showed me just how much I needed to get my power back.

In a massive turn of events, my outlet became my awakening. My lowest point became the stepping-stone. And my reflection became the realization.

'In case I never told you...' became my savior.

To My Depression

In case I never told you, you're like a bad simile.
You make the curtains become a wall, blocking
out any ray of sunlight trying to come through.
You make the sheets on my bed feel like
restraints holding me down.
You make the comfiest pillows more like a
microphone I used to scream into.

In case I never told you, when you come around
all hope is lost.
My hopes for a brighter tomorrow
Lost.
My hopes that this will pass
Lost.

My hopes that someone will finally understand,

Lost.

In case I never told you, you make me feel so
weak.
Weak because I let one thing stop me from
achieving my better tomorrow.
Weak because I can't seem to find the strength to
pick myself up.
Weak because I really don't see or want to see the
point anymore.

In case I never told you, when I think it can't get
any worse, you partner with anxiety and remind that it
can.
And it will.
The two of you take away what little optimism I
have left.
You remind me I'm not as strong as I thought.
You both seem to want to knock me off of
whatever pedestal I find myself on.

In case I never told you, one day I'll be able to

rewrite the bad similes.

One day I'll be able to open the curtains and let

the light back in.

One day I'll break out of your restraints.

One day the microphone will be put on mute.

In case I never told you, emotions were intended

to be controlled.

Not consumed.

I might not have full control today, but one day I

will.

One day you will be another battle I overcame

Self-Reflection

To My Anxiety

In case I never told you, you have a way of
morphing my reality—
Making hyperventilation seem like the only form
of breathing—
Fear appears to be the only emotion—
Negativity the only way of thinking.

In case I never told you, your presence is always
known.
Even when not physically there, you can push out
all other emotion and become the center of attention.
In one split second you can create panic and a
sense of helplessness.
Any situation you are able, you take control over.

In case I never told you, it's scary what you can

do to me—

Making the most organized person feel so

unprepared—

Making the adventurous turn timid—

Turning the optimist into the new pessimist.

In case I never told you, I'm going to gain control

again.

I NEED to gain control again.

I can no longer let you dictate how my day is

going to go.

I can no longer let you make me fearful of the

future I used to be so excited to see.

In case I never told you, I will learn how to

conquer my anxiety.

SELF-REFLECTION

To the Girl Looking In the Mirror

In case I never told you, you're more than this
reflection;
A distorted image altered by the way you think
you need to look.
That look is not you;
You are beautiful as is.
Is it worth the self-hate to keep looking in the
mirror?
The same mirror you see only flaws magnified?
You are not flawed;
Society's expectations are flawed.

In case I never told you, it's okay to want to look
a certain way.
However, when that look becomes an obsession,
you lose all boundaries to achieve,
That's when it's no longer okay.
It is okay to be you, I promise.
I promise, you won't know true beauty until you
see it in yourself.
No look is worth the countless meals replaced
with one more mile on the treadmill.
What you define as beautiful is in fact flawed.

In case I never told you, you are not ugly.
What is ugly is your willingness to allow your
self-worth to be based off a swipe to the right.
Right now, you're confused—
Confusing opinions for value.

In case I never told you, you might not love you,
But someone out there does.
Does their opinion matter?
Does it matter that you are killing yourself to
gain approval from people who haven't thought twice

about how their comments contributed to your self-
hatred?

In case I never told you, you need help;
You need help to see what beauty is.
You need help understanding that it is okay to be
called beautiful
Not only on the inside, but also on the outside
Don't let the outside beauty be the only beautiful
thing that matters.

In case I never told you, look in the mirror;
Though when you look this time, I want you to
see the person looking back at you
Not the image.
You don't see yourself for what you are because
you allow the ugliness of self-hate to expose itself on
the surface.
To the girl looking in the mirror, I want you to
love you.

SELF-REFLECTION

To My 'Because of You'

In case I never told you, because of you, I
struggle with my image.
I constantly wonder if the reflection looking back
at me in the mirror is the same image being seen in
everyone's eyes.
If it is, I can partially blame that for being the
reason why I won't be their type too.

In case I never told you, because of you, I stop
trying before I start.
I stop myself from attempting because every
attempt with you I failed
And if I fail again, I don't know if I'll have the
courage to try again.

In case I never told you, because of you, I'm
afraid.
So afraid that they'll find the same flaws
unbearable and leave.
If they leave that's another door closing without
the cliché 'another one opening'

In case I never told you, because of you, I think
it's better to just change all the locks on these
countless closing doors.
Because if I change the locks, no one can get in.
If no one can get in, no one can leave
And if no one leaves I can't get hurt.

In case I never told you, because of you, I believe
I'm destined to be alone.
After all, if I can't love me, how can they?
And if they do love me, how can I possibly
believe it?

In case I never told you, because of you, "I love
you" has lost its meaning.

Instead, "I love you" became the new synonym
for "I'm sorry",
And "I'm sorry" lost its meaning directly after "I
promise" did.

In case I never told you, because of you, Mr.
Right is sounding like the fictional Prince Charming
in all the fairy tales
And I have come to the realization that fairy tales
aren't real.

In case I never told you, because of you, I
compare myself to all of your first choices.
And if I'm comparing myself to them, I'll never
be perfect.

In case I never told you, because of you, I
wonder if what we had was lost love
Because you can't lose something you never truly
had.

Self-Reflection

To My Role Model

In case I never told you, I've heard it all.
I heard how tired you were in your voice
But never saw you stop.
I heard you crying through the door
But never saw the tears.
I heard you pray for help
But never saw the struggle.

In case I never told you, I watched it all.
I watched you go without just so I never had to.
I watched you make it look so effortless when
inside you were trying to figure it out yourself.

I watched you tell others you had it handled

when you were truly having a hard time making ends

meet.

In case I never told you, I always wanted to grow

up to be just like you.

But you wanted more for me,

So, you pushed me—

You pushed me to wipe my own tears because

you never wanted anyone to see me weak—

Pushed me to be humble for all I had because I

didn't know the sacrifices it took to get it—

You pushed me not to be discouraged and to

keep on problem solving.

In case I never told you, when I make it, you'll

never have to keep going when you're tired

Because it's my turn to work.

You'll never have to hide your tears

Because I'm here to wipe them.

You'll never have to pray for help

Because you're never going to go without.

In case I never told you, I know you wished you
could have done more.

But I'm here to tell you, I heard, I watched, and I
learned.

I learned that while others will never meet their
role models, I had mine in front of me the entire time.

I learned that to be half of the person you are
means I've made it.

Because of you I learned the definition of being
strong.

SELF-REFLECTION

To My Abandoner

In case I never told you, I am okay.
I am okay because I had them;
Them being the ones who could show the
unconditional love you couldn't;
Them being the ones that called just because;
Them being the ones that saw enough in me to
want to stay.

In case I never told you, I found my peace.
I found peace in your absence because I had their
presence.
In your absence, I found acceptance;
Acceptance that I cannot be everything everyone
wants me to be.

In your absence, I found my motivation;
Motivation that pushes me to never make a
commitment I don't plan to keep.
In your absence, I found a way to trust;
And with my trust in others, I earned theirs.
In your absence, I found appreciation;
Appreciation and gratitude for the ones who
stayed through the storms.

In case I never told you, I don't hate you
anymore.
I can't hate you for walking out because they let
me in instead;
I can't hate you because I made something out of
myself
And you missed that journey;
I can't hate you because I think you need this
more than I do.
I don't hate you because hatred, much like guilt,
will consume you and turn the sweetest of hearts
bitter.

In case I never told you, I forgive you.

I forgive you for leaving;

I forgive you for all the nights I stayed up

wondering why I wasn't enough for you to stay;

I forgive you for never calling;

I forgive you for not being there when I couldn't

admit I needed you to be;

In case I never told you, I forgave you in order to

save me.

SELF-REFLECTION

To the One Insisting on Being Independent

In case I never told you, it's going to get lonely;
Lonely doing everything on your own.
You think it makes you stronger,
But sometimes the strongest thing you can do is
let others help you.

In case I never told you, you don't have to do
everything on your own.
Swallow your pride and let others in.
Let others help you get to where you want to be.
There's no shame in that.

There's only shame in the goals you won't allow
yourself to reach because it requires others to become
involved.

In case I never told you, there's a difference
between independence and stubbornness.
The stubborn fall short.
The stubborn refuse to be met half way.
The stubborn will never be independent.
The independent are driven.
The independent strive.
The independent do not allow interference.

In case I never told you, help is not interference.
Help is finding others who have the same goals
and work to make the goal achievable.
Help is realizing that sometimes another entity is
needed.
Help doesn't make you vulnerable.

In case I never told you, don't waste your
potential because you confuse independence with
pride.

Pride will bring struggle.

Pride will bring losses.

Pride will bring missed opportunities.

37

In case I never told you, your definition of independence will only bring you heart break.

Self-Reflection

To the One Trying to Find the Light Again

In case I never told you, the world is cold,
So cold it can turn any heart into an icebox.
The type of icebox that requires a pickaxe to
break.

In case I never told you, take control of the
thermostat of your own life.
Promote the warmth you so desperately seek.
Let your body thaw.

In case I never told you, it takes more time to
freeze something than it does to thaw it.

Don't let the uncertainties of tomorrow freeze
you in your tracks.

In case I never told you, you have the flame
inside of you to melt through the ice wall the world
has created.
Let the flame melt the sheet of ice you find
yourself slipping on.
Because underneath every sheet of ice is a new
opportunity for growth.

In case I never told you, once that ice melts, the
flowers begin to grow again.
And just like the seasons, the winter of your life
is followed directly by sunshine.

Self-Reflection

To the One Who Lost Control

In case I never told you, I lost control of my own
life.

My life started to turn into a bad TV series
rerun... and I lost the remote.

Just like the rerun, my life felt like it couldn't be
changed.

The remote of my life was lost.

In case I never told you, what if I'm the one that
is lost?

What if I'm the remote that I once had a grip on,
but suddenly it's nowhere to be found?

What if in order to find what is lost, I have to
look deeper than what's on the surface?
Maybe I need to start picking myself up off the
couch cushions I find myself sinking deeper and
deeper, night after night.

In case I never told you, it might take more effort
than I have been willing to put in.
Effort I stopped putting in because I found
comfort.
I found comfort in my contentment.

In case I never told you, if we're not willing to do
something about our circumstances, that means they
aren't unbearable.
It's not until something becomes unbearable, that
we as humans find the desire to change.

In case I never told you, I need to change.
I need to pick myself up from the cliff I let
myself go over.
After all, rolling took less effort than climbing.

The steepness and pressure that came with my
goals became too much.
So, I let myself fall.

In case I never told you, I'm ready to climb.
But this time when I climb, I'm going to have
support.
I'm going to have my crutch to help me when the
steepness and pressure get to be too much.
In case I never told you, I may stumble during
this climb, but I'll never fall.

SELF-REFLECTION

TO MY WISH

In case I never told you, you are what I wish for
on the first star I see at night.
A selfish part of me I cannot seem to shake.

In case I never told you, I want to experience true
happiness—
A happiness that has no expiration—
A happiness that when others see me, they hope
to find the reason I'm smiling for themselves—
A happily ever after to my own story.

In case I never told you, my story is constantly
being rewritten and edited.
But it's okay.

It's okay to be at this age and not have it all
figured out.
It's okay to go through trials and errors.
It's okay to keep wishing on the stars.

In case I never told you, the happily ever after
you wished for yourself might only be one chapter to
your life's story.
It is possible that the true happiness you wish for
yourself is only a percentage of the final happiness
you will get in your lifetime.
It's possible you are trying to rush a good thing.

In case I never told you, it's important to practice
patience.
Just because the time feels right, does not mean
it's the right timing.

In case I never told you, keep wishing, keep
reaching, and keep seeking.

Self-Reflection

To the Ones That Stepped Up

In case I never told you, you stepped up when
you didn't have to.
You fixed mistakes you didn't make.
You made it clear I never had to do anything on
my own.
You showed me that sometimes water can be
thicker than blood.

In case I never told you, I'm grateful you were
there.
I'm grateful you were there to tell me "no."
I'm grateful you were there to teach me the things
the ones who left didn't.

I'm grateful you had my back when it seemed
like no one else did.

In case I never told you, I don't know how to
repay you for that.
I feel like nothing I can do will amount to all you
did for me.
I feel like no words can express how much you
mean to me.
You deserve more than I could ever give.

In case I never told you, it takes a special person
to do what you did.
It takes someone mature to fix the things they did
not break.
Someone patient to wait for their love to be
reciprocated.
It takes someone non-judgmental to understand
how much the others had an effect on me.

In case I never told you, I love you for all you
have done.

SELF-REFLECTION

To the One the World Is Trying to Change

In case I never told you, don't.

Don't let other's hatred consume you.

Don't let other's mistreatment of you affect your
treatment of those around you.

Don't let their actions change your outlook on the
world.

In case I never told you, there are people in this
world like you—

People in this world who deal with a version, if
not the same, mistreatment but will never show it—

People in this world who have been hurt a time
or two but never let it permanently bruise their
hearts—
People in this world who gave out one too many
second chances but will still give out another to the
deserving.

In case I never told you, it makes you special—
Special that you continue to see the good in a
world that has limited amounts of it—
Special that you read, listen, and live His
teachings—
Special because you have a will others try to
break, but they can't.

In case I never told you, you don't need to
change.
Live the life you want to live.
Be a person you can be proud to look at in the
mirror daily.
Prove to everyone the world is trying to change
that they are not alone.

In case I never told you, show everyone that
good can win.

54

SELF-REFLECTION

To the One I Couldn't Save

In case I never told you, it's too hard to watch—
Too hard to watch you find comfort in the one
thing that's killing you slowly—
Too hard to watch you choose this over us—
Too hard to watch you let yourself self-destruct.

In case I never told you, I prayed every night.
I prayed that one day it really would be your last
time.
I prayed you would reach the epiphany that you
don't need this to function day to day.
I prayed that you would find another way.

In case I never told you, you are not you
anymore.
You are not the person I once knew.
You are not the person who used to bring joy to a
room as soon as you walked in.
You are not the same person people could rely
on.

In case I never told you, if you won't do it for
you, please do it for them.
Please look into the eyes of the ones you love
and see their pain.
Take a step back and see the harm you're causing
yourself.
Please, listen when we say you're better than this.

In case I never told you, I'm afraid it's going to be
too late—
Too late before you quit and no longer have the
chance to wake up each morning—
Too late before you decide you love us more than
this and we're all gone—

Too late before you find another way to deal with
your pain and you just become numb to any sort of
feelings at all.

In case I never told you, I hope one day you can
break this addiction.
Because right now, I don't know what hurts
worse
The idea of a world without you in it
Or a world that doesn't have the real you in it.

SELF-REFLECTION

To the One Looking For Acceptance

In case I never told you, you might not think
you're perfect,
But you're perfect in someone else's eyes.
So perfect that it kills them to watch you be your
own demise.

In case I never told you, I think you're scared—
So scared to be good at something,
You'll stop yourself from seeing anything
through.

In case I never told you, you don't have to be
reluctant—

Reluctant to put yourself first when all you ever
do is prioritize others—
Reluctant to follow the advice you so carefully
choose to give—
Reluctant to dream big for fear your dreams were
too big.

In case I never told you, you're dimming your
own light—
The light that once made you, you.
When did you stop shining and start subduing?

In case I never told you, you're insecure—
Insecure to the point you belittle yourself.
You have flaws, but you can make them
beautiful.
You underestimate your potential daily.

In case I never told you, it is time to start—
Start recognizing before criticizing—
Start embracing before shaming—
Start living before just existing.

In case I never told you, you've been looking for
acceptance in the wrong places
And searching for acceptance from the wrong
people.
In case I never told you, the one who needs to
accept you—is you.

SELF-REFLECTION

To the Ones Who Weren't Meant to Be Permanent

In case I never told you, you weren't meant to be

permanent.

You were meant to be a temporary figure in my

life to convey a lesson—

A lesson with a purpose—

A purpose for coming into my life,

And a purpose for leaving it.

In case I never told you, from the time you came,

to the time you left, you taught me something;

Something that at the time wasn't clear;

Something still to this day that might not be fully

clear to me yet.

In you leaving, you fulfilled your purpose that

helped to complete me.

In case I never told you, I don't resent you.

How could I resent you for defining your own

standards?

Standards I couldn't conform to,

Because by conforming to them, I'd lose myself,

And losing myself would have been the greater

loss.

In case I never told you, I'm sorry.

I'm sorry I couldn't be what you wanted me to be.

I'm sorry you set expectations—

Expectations that weren't right for me.

I'm sorry you are not here—

Not here to see what I've become.

In case I never told you, I think about you from

time to time.

At times I need a reminder—

A reminder of where I was.

A place I don't want to go back to;

To go back means I stop going forward—
Forward to the expectations I set for myself,
Expectations that are right for me.

In case I never told you, I am glad you weren't
meant to stay.

SELF-REFLECTION

TO THE LAST TIME

In case I never told you, this was the last time.
The last time I'm going to feel so low and
ashamed
Ashamed of the fact I thought you could change.

In case I never told you, you're never going to
change.
So, I have to.
I have to realize you became too comfortable.
Too comfortable with the power you were given.

In case I never told you, I'm taking my power
back.
The power I gave you to manipulate me.

The power I gave you to use me.
The power I gave you to hurt me time and time
again.

In case I never told you, I'm done crying.
I'm done crying over something you did.
I'm done praying God sends me a sign to know
the truth about you, when he's already sent plenty.
I'm done believing you didn't mean to do it.

In case I never told you, I know you meant it.
I know you meant it all.
And because of that, I have to let you go.
I'm letting you go because anyone who could
intentionally do this to someone doesn't deserve me.
I'm letting you go because I know I deserve
better.
I'm letting you go because I finally realize you
bring no positivity to my life.

In case I never told you, you're a parasite
Feeding off of me.

Letting me deal with the consequences while you
reap the rewards
Taking all you can from me until you can't
anymore.

In case I never told you, you can't anymore.

Self-Reflection

To the Ones With Thoughts of Ending It All

In case I never told you, you're my biggest secret.
A secret I keep hidden from the world.

In case I never told you, no one knows.
No one knows the constant fight I have with you;
The fight to be stronger than the solutions inside
my head.
No one knows how far it's gone;
So far gone I don't know how to see the good
anymore.
So far gone I lost sight of the light;
A light that used to be at the end of even the
longest tunnels.

In case I never told you, I was losing my will;
My will to keep fighting;
Fighting a fight that I seemed to be losing for far
too long.
A fight that became too frequent.
So frequent that I became too familiar with
feeling misery.

In case I never told you, I prayed for you to go
away.
I prayed one day to be strong again—
Strong enough to see my own strength.
I prayed one day self-harm would not be the
answer.

In case I never told you, I wanted to give up.
But I found my faith again.
My faith in God—
My faith in His plan—
A plan I am not close to completing.

In case I never told you, I need to keep going.

You need to keep going.

Self-Reflection

To This Book

In case I never told you, thank you for helping
me let go—
Let go of all the negative consuming my life—
Let go of the baggage that has been weighing me
down—
Let go of the entities in my life that I was
allowing to control it.

In case I never told you, you have become my
outlet—
An outlet I never expected to find.
By finding you, you helped me find myself.
By finding you, you helped me find a source for
all the pain—

Pain I suppressed for far too long.

In case I never told you, writing you scared me.
It scared me because I had to face issues I have
been neglecting.
It scared me because I was letting myself be
vulnerable.
It scared me because this inner battle I've been
fighting will now be shared with others.

In case I never told you, you are helping me face
my demons—
Demons who I let take away everything:
My energy
My strength
My confidence
My hope.

In case I never told you, you might have saved
my life.
You helped me find peace in all the wrongs.
You helped me find motivation when it was lost.

Ashleigh Peroney

You helped me realize something beautiful can
come from all the struggles.

SELF-REFLECTION

To My Failures

In case I never told you, I'm grateful for you.
I'm grateful that you were there to stop me from
achieving things—
The wrong things.
The things you knew weren't right for me.

In case I never told you, thank you.
Thank you for keeping me humble—
Humble in the sense that I take none of my
accomplishments for granted.

In case I never told you, I appreciate you.
I appreciate the fact that you were my warning
sign—

A warning sign to show me there might be
another way—
A warning sign to give me direction.
I appreciate you for being my drive—
A drive that pushed me to be better—
A drive that pushed me to work harder.
I appreciate you for being my re-evaluation—
A re-evaluation on my wants—
A re-evaluation on my priorities.

In case I never told you, you were my greatest
lesson.
You taught me how not to be perfect.
And you taught me that was okay.
Without you, my successes would not be as
rewarding—
Rewarding in that I figured out why you were in
my path in the first place.
You were there to help mold me.

In case I never told you, while you may have
helped mold me,
You will never define me.

SELF-REFLECTION

TO MY FAITH

In case I never told you, I'm sorry I let other
things come between us—
Letting my weakness alter my need for you—
Letting my fear of the unknown question you—
Letting my naive mind lead me to believe you
had failed me.
Despite all that, I always found my way back to
you.

In case I never told you, I am nothing without
you.
Because I know without you, I will always
lose—
I'll lose every battle thrown at me.

You keep me strong when I feel weak.
Grounded when I feel pushed.
You give me reason when I seek answers.

In case I never told you, you're the reason I'm
still here—
Here to see another day—
Here to overcome another obstacle—
Here to help another—
Another searching for answers—
Another being pushed to their limits—
Another needing to be reminded of their strength.

In case I never told you, you are my saving
grace—
Saving me from the harsh reality of the world—
Saving me from myself.

In case I never told you, I need you.
I need you to continue to guide me.
I need you to continue to find your way back to
me.

I need you to continue to help me find and
understand my purpose.
In case I never told you, I will never lose faith
again.

SELF-REFLECTION

To The Girl Who Hurts Herself

In case I never told you, I know you're tired—
Tired of the pain—
Pain you have become all too familiar with.
But this pain you feel is only temporary.
The scars will be forever—
There to keep you in the past—
A past, which you need to leave behind.

In case I never told you, I understand.
I understand the emotional pain can be too
much—
So much so that you prefer the physical pain to
escape—

Escape from the emotional pain you can't bear,
even if it is an escape for just a minute,
Because even just a minute is worth it.

In case I never told you, you are special—
So special that you're still here—
Here to complete your purpose for this world—
A world that needs you in it.

In case I never told you, you are strong—
Stronger than this.
This pain consuming you, you can overcome it.
Because you have overcome—
Overcoming every obstacle thrown your way
thus far.

In case I never told you, it will get better—
Better than it has ever been.
You have been through a lot—
Some of which seemed impossible,
But you managed to make it through.

In case I never told you, nothing is impossible for you.

89

SELF-REFLECTION

TO MY USER

In case I never told you, you broke me.
You broke me and I let you.
I let you make me feel that I was doing the right
thing by giving you everything;
I let you live in comfort while I struggled day to
day;
I let you think it was okay.

In case I never told you, none of it was okay.
It was never okay to start a conversation with a
request;
It was never okay for you to make me only feel
worth something when I gave you everything;

It was never okay to take advantage of someone
who would do anything to make sure that you never
had to know how it felt to struggle;
It was never okay that while I was losing sleep
trying to figure out how to help you, you had no
doubts that I'd find a way;
It was never okay that I built a wall and started to
lose my faith in humanity.

In case I never told you, even though you broke
me, I still want to thank you.
Thank you for bringing the harsh reality that
some people in this world have ulterior motives;
Thank you for opening my eyes to the fact that
the world is not full of people like me—
People who could never be okay with an
individual going without just to ensure I could go
with—
People who would exert themselves to provide
for themselves before going to someone else's aide—
People who want to earn rather than be given—
People who know the meaning of sacrifice—
People who are genuine.

In case I never told you, I never want to be like
you—
You, who looks for handouts rather than hard
work—
You, who can day by day never amount to
anything—
You, who will be met by karma one day—
You, who may have everything, but will never
truly be happy.

In case I never told you, I may have let you break
me once, but you never will again.

SELF-REFLECTION

To My Next Love

In case I never told you, please be patient—
Patient while I try to find the me that I lost while
being with them—
Patient while I try to build back the confidence I
let them take away—
Patient while I try to trust again.

In case I never told you, I will frustrate you.
I will say sorry when it's not needed, because
they trained me to think I was always wrong.
I will question if I'm really good enough, because
I wasn't for them.
I will doubt all your motives, because theirs were
ulterior.

In case I never told you, I will try to push you
away.
I'll push you away because I'm scared it's too
good to be true.
I'll push you away because I'll think you could do
better.
I'll push you away before you can hurt me too.

In case I never told you, if you wait this out, I
will love you.
I will never have you questioning that I'm yours.
I will show you a new definition of love.
I will give you all of me.

In case I never told you, I hope you're the one.
The one who can help me find myself.
The one who will have enough confidence in me
for the both of us.
The one I can put my trust in.

In case I never told you, I'm ready to believe in
love again.

SELF-REFLECTION

To My Unconventional Love

In case I never told you, you were the love I
never saw coming.
The love I wasn't looking for, but somehow
found.
The type of love that had me doing things I never
thought I would.
The type of love that made me the type of person
I didn't want to be.

In case I never told you, you were an
unconventional love.
Love that had me accepting the once
unacceptable.

The type of love that made me sick, but I
couldn't get sick of.
Pain is pleasure, but pleasure is pain kind of love.

In case I never told you, you were an
unconventional love.
Love I turned my back on, but always seemed to
be facing head on.
Love that put you in the uncomfortable situations
I somehow found myself finding comfort in.
The type of love I wanted to walk out on, but had
my feet glued to the ground.

In case I never told you, you were an
unconventional love.
The love I cried myself to sleep over.
The love I couldn't sleep because of.
The love that had me so tired but had me so
awake at the same time.

In case I never told you, you were an
unconventional love.
Love that made me cold while it warmed me too.

The type of love that made no sense, but all the
sense in the world.
The oxymoron of love.

100

In case I never told you, you were an
unconventional love.

SELF-REFLECTION

To My 'If Only I Knew'

In case I never told you, if only I knew, you
would be someone I was going to enjoy being around;
Someone I was going to care for;
Someone I would fall in love with;
Someone I would overcome unthinkable battles
with
Not knowing that eventually there would be one
battle we wouldn't win.

In case I never told you, if only I knew, you were
going to be someone I feel sick when I'm not around;
Someone I would lose sleep over;
Someone who would completely break my heart;

In case I never told you, if only I knew all of these things, I would have still loved you anyway.

SELF-REFLECTION

To the Ones Who Gave Up on Me

In case I never told you, the fact that you gave up
on me makes me feel badly—
Not for me, but for you.
You're going to be hearing about my
accomplishments from a third party.
You're never going to get the opportunity to
share in my successes.
You're never going to get the chance to
experience the beauty of the rainbow,
All because you couldn't wait out the storm.
You're only going to be able to speak about our
journey together in the past tense.

In case I never told you, the moment you gave up
on me was the moment I gained another piece of
motivation—
Motivation to prove that I was worth weathering
the storm—
Motivation to show you all my dreams will
become reality—
Motivation to not let your inability to see my true
potential outshine the ones who have seen it from the
beginning.

In case I never told you, a weight has been
lifted—
The weight that was pulling me back—
The weight I was wasting time trying to convince
to keep fighting with me—
The weight that was making me sink.

In case I never told you, I found my anchor.
The anchor that makes everything seem less
heavy.
The anchor that is helping me rise to the top.

And one day, you're going to wish you had stayed.

Self-Reflection

TO MY CHOICE

In case I never told you, I chose my sanity.

I chose to stop letting the negativity of us stop
me from living.

I chose accepting that if you're going to leave,
you will

Regardless if I beg you not to.

I chose to stop looking for proof that my gut
feeling is wrong when it hasn't been yet.

In case I never told you, I chose to accept the
love I believe I deserve.

I chose to try until I can't try anymore.

I chose silence because I want to find my
strength.

In case I never told you, I chose your happiness

over mine for far too long.

I chose to stop believing I needed you to keep

going.

I chose to risk my heart.

In case I never told you, I'm choosing for myself

SELF-REFLECTION

To My Obstacles

In case I never told you, you delayed my
progress,
Although you were never able to stop it.
You may have blindsided me a time or two,
But I was always able to find my way—
My way around you—
My way to overcome you.

In case I never told you, you seemed impossible
countless times,
But countless times, I proved nothing is ever
impossible for me—
Me, who has a vision—

Me, who has the will to fight for anything worth
having.

In case I never told you, you showed me how
badly I wanted to reach my goals.
You showed me I was able to give more than the
all I thought I did before.
You showed me my determination—
Determination to never let anything stop me from
becoming the person *He* intended me to be.

In case I never told you, I hope you keep coming.
I hope you keep coming so I can continue to
prove myself—
To prove that I'm stronger than any obstacle.

Self-Reflection

To the Ones Who Are Envious

In case I never told you, you have your own
opportunities—
Opportunities to do something great—
Something great that's all your own.

In case I never told you, don't waste time wishing
you had what they had.
Take the time you're wasting and focus it—
Focus it on pursuing your own:
Your own success,
Your own goals,
Your own life.

In case I never told you, you'll never be them.
God made you to be you—
Your own person—
Your own person who has their own path to
follow.

In case I never told you, as soon as you lose the
envy, you'll realize life can be something more—
More than the bitterness you let spew from your
mouth when you speak about others—
More than the sore you put in your eyes when
you see others succeed—
More than the hatred you let consume your own
heart—

In case I never told you, envy will always leave a
void.
As long as you're envious, you'll never be able to
fill it.
As long as you're envious, you'll never feel
whole.
As long as you're envious, you'll be missing out
on all that has been offered to you.

In case I never told you, it's time to focus on
what really matters:
YOU.

SELF-REFLECTION

To My 'It's Never Too Late'

In case I never told you, it might not have
happened when it was intended to,
But it happened when it was supposed to.
Sometimes the intended time just wasn't the right
time.
It's a force greater than us controlling the timing
of everything.

In case I never told you, it might not have
happened then,
But it's happening now.
So, let's live in the moment and not worry about
the past.
Living in the past will only stop our future.

In case I never told you, everyone has a "day one".

Let's make today ours.

Our day one started the day you came back.

Our day one started when you became bigger than your mistake.

Our day one started when you proved yourself stronger than the "what if" scenario you put in your head.

Our day one started when you stopped living in fear.

Self-Reflection

TO MY 'IT WAS JUST ONE TIME'

In case I never told you, you traded down.
You traded a beautiful soul for a beautiful face.
You traded your ride or die chick for no more
than a ride.
You traded a happily ever after for a happy
ending.

In case I never told you, the one you traded in is
going to be just fine.
There is beauty in their flaws.
The ride might be bumpy, but it eventually leads
to paradise.
Their chapters might have turning points, but it's
a book someone will want to read till the end.

In case I never told you, it might have been just
one night to you.
But it wasn't to me.
That "random fuck"
Well, it fucked me up.
That "it'll never happen again"
It plays in my head every night.

In case I never told you, you did this to us.
You cut off a person who wanted to show you
the beauty in your own flaws.
You ended a journey before it ever got to start.
You closed the book before reaching the climax.

In case I never told you, this is one time you
can't take back.

SELF-REFLECTION

To My Lie

In case I never told you, I lied.
I lied when I said I was fine.
I lied when I said I'll be ok.
I lied when I acted like I wasn't fazed.
I lied when I said I've handled this before
Truth is, I've never experienced love like you
before.

In case I never told you, I wish I could lie and
say you meant nothing.
I wish I could say I didn't love someone who
didn't love me back.
Each debate on what you wanted took away any
confidence I had built up in us.

In case I never told you, we never saw the same
things.
How can I love someone who doesn't love me
back?
How can I see perfection and you see a life
where you live without me?
Why do I see happiness but all you feel is
misery?
Why can your bad decisions be forgiven but
mine constantly haunt me?
Why can't I let you go like you have done to me?
Why did I let myself believe you were in denial?
Why did I let myself be an option again?
Why can't I just let go?

In case I never told you, I lied when I said I don't
love you anymore.

SELF-REFLECTION

To My 'Make Her Feel Special'

In case I never told you, remember to make her
feel special.

Rotations like clockwork.

Routines on the daily.

Doing theirs rounds checking in with each.

In case I never told you, remember to make her
feel special.

Copy and pasting responses because it's easier
than retyping it three times.

Kiss one goodbye.

Kiss the next hello.

In case I never told you, remember to make her
feel special.
Having their main, their loyal one, and their one
who is fun.
Have the ones they like, but not wanting to truly
invest in one.

In case I never told you, remember to make her
feel special.
Providing none with status so they can leave at
any time.
Providing none with status so they can keep them
while they find the one who they'll give the status to.

In case I never told you, remember none of them
are really special.

SELF-REFLECTION

To My Abuser

In case I never told you, you raised your hand
Not to question anything, but to put me in my
place.
You grabbed me,
Not to hold me, but to have a hold on me.
You talked at me, not to me.
You said, "You're beautiful", not to me, but to
her.
You said, "You won't ever be enough", not to
her, but to me.
You told me to put on makeup,
Not to take me out, but to cover up the marks.
You said you would stop, but you never did.
I was silent,

Not because I had nothing to say, but because
you never heard me anyway.
I walked behind you,
Not because you were the leader, but because
you trained me to believe you were.
I walked with my head down,
Not because I was looking at something, but
because you saw through me anyway.
You destroyed me for long enough,
Not because you had the power, but because I let
you.

In case I never told you, I'm not letting you hurt
me anymore.

Self-Reflection

To My Feeling

In case I never told you, it's the feeling of being
alone when you're not.
The feeling of never being able to express your
pain because you just contribute to someone's
annoyance.
The feeling that if I share this part of me it won't
make a difference.
The feeling of praying to have someone to talk
to, but once you talk you feel worse.
The feeling of that don't have time to cope
because you have other people to please.
The feeling that you must let go but you hold on
so tight because they just need a little more time.

In case I never told you, it's the feeling that no one loves you as much as you love them.

The feeling of trying to convince someone you're worth being in love with.

The feeling of exhaustion trying to convince them.

The feeling of knowing the truth when you don't want to believe it.

The feeling of hating the heart you were given because it has too much love for the things that just don't feel the same.

The feeling of constantly failing.

The feeling of always being in the wrong.

The feeling of doubting all the choices you make.

The feeling of anxiety, yet you can't pin-point the cause.

The feeling of worthlessness.

The feeling of heaviness.

The feeling of darkness consuming you.

The feeling of finally being ready to give up.

The feeling of being tired of being the one showing fight.

The feeling of letting yourself down.

In case I never told you, it's the feeling of
watching yourself do everything you told yourself
you'll never do again.
The feeling of waiting for someone to love you
back.
The feeling of wondering what its purpose was.
The feeling of feeling yourself slipping again.
The feeling of already knowing the outcome, but
praying you're wrong.

In case I never told you, it's the feeling of panic.
The feeling of 'Am I giving up to soon?'
The feeling of being buried alive and no one
being there to dig you out.
The feeling of needing more, but not thinking
you deserve it.
The feeling of holding onto the few good times,
hoping they'll eventually outweigh the bad.
The feeling of 'Maybe I'm being too sensitive.'

In case I never told you, it's the feeling of too
many feelings you can't feel at all.

SELF-REFLECTION

In case I never told you…the story is not over.